WE WILL NOT BE SILENT

Hans Scholl, Sophie Scholl, and Christoph Probst, founding members of the White Rose student resistance movement in Nazi Germany. Munich, June 1942.

WE WILL NOT BE SILENT

THE WHITE ROSE
STUDENT RESISTANCE MOVEMENT
THAT DEFIED ADOLF HITLER

RUSSELL FREEDMAN

CLARION BOOKS

HOUGHTON MIFFLIN HARCOURT

BOSTON • NEW YORK

Many thanks to Alfons Balthesen, who helped guide me through the
collections of the White Rose Museum; Stella Calvert-Smith of akg
images; Caroline Waddell of the United States Memorial Holocaust
Museum; James Cross Giblin for sharing his insights concerning
the Hitler regime; and Evans Chan, who photographed White Rose
landmarks throughout Munich especially for this book.

TO DINAH STEVENSON

······ CONTENTS ······

★★★★★★ PREFACE ★★★★★★

In 1942, when World War II was in its third year, leaflets began to appear mysteriously in mailboxes all over Nazi Germany. Someone would open an envelope, pull out a leaflet, take one look, then turn and glance around nervously to make sure no one was watching. A person could not be too careful. Anyone caught with a seditious leaflet was marked as an enemy of the state and could land in a concentration camp, or worse.

Neatly typed, run off on a mimeograph machine, these documents were headed "Leaflets of the White Rose." They assailed the Nazi "dictatorship of evil," denounced Adolf Hitler as a liar and blasphemer, and called on the German people to rise up and overthrow the Nazi regime.

Where were these inflammatory leaflets coming from? Who was the White Rose? Was more than one person involved? The Nazi secret police, the Gestapo, organized a special task force to hunt down those responsible. A reward was offered for information leading to their "speedy arrest."

The hunt for the White Rose finally led to Munich, the cradle of the Nazi government.

Members of the Deutsches Jungvolk (German Young Folk), the boys' junior division of the Hitler Youth, pound their drums at a Nazi Party rally in Nuremberg, Germany.

ONE

EMBRACED BY THE HITLER YOUTH

HANS Scholl held his head high and his eyes fixed straight ahead as he stepped forward smartly, marching shoulder to shoulder with his comrades in the Hitler Youth.

Against his father's wishes, Hans had joined the Hitler Youth movement when he was fourteen. His father, Robert, was opposed to Germany's new leader, Adolf Hitler, and his National Socialist, or Nazi, political party. "Don't believe them," he warned his children. "They are wolves and deceivers, and they are misusing the German people shamefully." But Hitler had promised the nation's young people that they would be the architects of a glorious future, and Hans wanted to be a part of that noble cause.

Hitler Youth recruiting poster. The text reads: YOUTH
SERVES THE FÜHRER/ALL TEN-YEAR-OLDS INTO THE HITLER YOUTH.

Werner. "We entered into it with body and soul," Inge recalled, "and we could not understand why our father did not approve."

Few youngsters growing up in Germany during the 1930s could resist the lure of the Hitler Youth movement, and the Scholl children were typical of their times. They were attracted by the uniforms that set each member apart as someone special, by the closed ranks of marching youth keeping time to drumbeat and song with flags and banners waving, by the feeling of belonging, the embracing sense of fellowship on hikes and camping trips.

"We heard much oratory about the fatherland, comradeship, . . . and love of country," Inge wrote. "This was impressive, and we listened closely. . . . They told us that we must dedicate our lives to a great cause. We were taken seriously . . . in a remarkable way — and that aroused our enthusiasm."

Robert Scholl tried to convince his children that no good could come of Hitler's promises. But his arguments were swept away by their youthful enthusiasm, and he granted them the right to choose. Hans had been the first to join, followed in turn by his three sisters, Inge, Elisabeth, and Sophie, and finally by their younger brother,

Membership was voluntary at first. Boys could enroll in the Young Folk when they were ten, then transfer to the Hitler Youth proper at fourteen. Girls joined the Young Maidens at ten, then the League of German Girls at fourteen. Later, membership became mandatory for all boys and girls of proven "Aryan" descent. Parents who kept

Adolf Hitler meets with a Hitler Youth troop, 1933.

their children from joining faced a heavy prison sentence.

Jewish youngsters, along with others of "inferior" ancestry, were not allowed to join. Hitler had declared that the "Aryan race," of which Germans were the supreme example, was the "master race," superior to all others.

Hitler had come to power in 1933, a time of political and economic turmoil. Germany had been defeated in World War I (1914–18). The peace terms dictated by the victorious Allies — Britain, France, Italy, and the United States — held the German people responsible for starting the war. Germany was required by this Treaty of Versailles to disarm, to give up certain territories, and to pay enormous amounts of

Shouting *"Heil Hitler!"* (Hail Hitler!), members of the Reichstag, the German parliament, salute their Führer, or Supreme Leader, Berlin, 1938. By the time this photograph was taken, Hitler had established himself as Germany's absolute dictator.

money, called reparations, as compensation for all the destruction and losses the war had caused.

Many Germans found these peace terms humiliating, and the reparations payments — more than could ever be paid — an unjust burden. The democratic Weimar Republic, the system of government established in Germany at the war's end, became a chaotic political battleground as some fifty warring parties failed to agree and the government failed to govern.

The worldwide economic depression that began in 1929 dealt Germany a heavy blow, causing widespread unemployment and a soaring rate of inflation. People lost their jobs and often their lifetime savings. All of this — the rankling feelings of humiliation, the anger and fear, the economic hardship and uncertainty — set the stage for Adolf Hitler's rise to power.

Hitler, a scrawny World War I corporal with a black toothbrush mustache and, as he would demonstrate, a hypnotic speaking manner, promised to create jobs and restore Germany's prosperity and military might. In his memoir *Mein Kampf* (My Struggle) and in his speeches, he claimed that Germans, or "Aryans," were destined to rule Europe.

Hitler convinced enough voters that he had the answers to Germany's problems to lead the Nazi Party to victory in the election of November 1932. Backed by his black-shirted storm troopers, who terrorized some political rivals and murdered others, Hitler rapidly established himself as Germany's absolute dictator — the Führer, or Supreme Leader. His portrait went up on the wall of every classroom and public building. Schoolchildren started the day with their right arms rigidly extended in the Nazi salute, shouting *"Heil Hitler!"* (Hail Hitler!). To criticize the Führer, or simply repeat a joke making fun of him, was an offense that could result in prison or even a death sentence.

During these years, the five Scholl children were growing up in Ulm, a cozy town on the Danube River, nestled among the valleys and mountains of Bavaria in the south of Germany. "Ulm — the name sounded to us like the boom of the biggest bell in the mighty cathedral," Inge Scholl recalled. The family had a big apartment facing Cathedral Square. Their windows looked across the square to the spires of the four-hundred-year-old Catholic cathedral.

Robert Scholl had been elected mayor of two small towns before moving his family to Ulm, where, even during the Depression years, he made a comfortable living as an attorney and financial adviser. He met his wife, Magdalene, a cheerful, devout woman, during the war at a German military hospital, where she worked as a nurse. Robert, a pacifist and conscientious objector, had refused to carry a gun and served instead as an army medic. He was as outspoken as his wife was soft-spoken.

When the Scholl children spoke of their "homeland," they usually meant the beautiful countryside around Ulm. "For we loved our land dearly — the woods, the river, the old gray stone

Robert Scholl with his children: Inge, Hans, Elisabeth, Sophie, and Werner. Ludwigsburg, Germany, 1930/1931.

Ulm, Germany, with the Ulm Cathedral in the background.

fences running along the steep slopes between orchards and vineyards," Inge wrote. "Every inch of it was familiar and dear. Our fatherland — what was it but the extended home of all those who shared a language and belonged to one people. We loved it, though we couldn't say why."

Sophie, perhaps the best writer in the family, put it this way: "I can never look at a limpid stream without at least dangling my feet in it; in the same way, I cannot walk past a meadow in May. . . . I lie in the grass, quite still, my arms spread, my knees raised, and am happy. Through the blossoming branches of an apple tree I see the blue sky. . . . When I turn my head, it touches the rough trunk. . . . I press my face to the tree's

dusky, warm bark and think, 'My homeland,' and I am inexpressibly grateful."

Hans, three years older than Sophie, was a natural leader. A few months after joining the Hitler Youth, he was promoted to the rank of squad leader and put in charge of 150 boys, one quarter of a larger group, a *Stamm*. He led his squad on long hikes and overnight camping trips, strummed his guitar and sang folk songs around evening campfires, and was always ready for the next new adventure. "Hans was a very complicated person, very special, different from other guys," a college friend recalled. "He saw different possibilities. On top of everything, Hans had no fear. He had no sense of danger. . . . If you

Ranks of Hitler Youth march through the streets of Nuremberg, 1935.

have no fear, you can have a clear vision. But it is dangerous."

In 1935, just before his seventeenth birthday, Hans was chosen to be the major flag bearer of the Ulm Hitler Youth contingent at a massive Nazi Party rally in Nuremberg. "Your Hans is so handsome," a friend told Inge. "He is the right boy to carry the flag of his *Stamm*." It was a great honor, and Hans was in high spirits as the flag-bedecked special train left the Ulm station for Nuremberg.

The rally, attended by 50,000 Nazi youths, was a spectacular weeklong celebration of speeches, marches, and torchlight processions. The Nazi Youth torchbearers sang as they marched along:

> We'll go on marching forever,
> Even if everything falls to pieces.

For today, Germany belongs to us —
And tomorrow the whole world.

The main events took place at a huge stadium circled by gigantic searchlights that shot brilliant beams into the night sky. On the last night of the rally, the searchlights highlighted the dramatic appearance of the Führer himself. A Nuremberg newspaper reported: "It seems that youth does not ever want to be silent again, for the Führer — their Führer — stands before the microphone to speak to them. Every time Adolf Hitler tries to begin, the endless cheers of *Heil!* roar again, subsiding only after minutes. Then the Führer speaks."

Standing at parade rest, Hans listened to every word that Hitler spoke. But Hans was troubled. The events of the past week had shaken his faith in the Führer and in his promises.

Hitler Youth flag bearers.

✳ ✳ ✳ ✳ TWO ✳ ✳ ✳ ✳

RUMBLINGS OF DOUBT

W HEN [Hans] returned, we could not believe our eyes," Inge recalled. "He looked tired and showed signs of a great disappointment."

Hans had been disillusioned by the mass conformity of the Nuremberg rally, the mindless obedience demanded of each participant. He had looked forward to an exciting experience, a chance to meet people and form new friendships. Instead there had been the lockstep regimentation of marches and drills, empty slogans, and deafening roars of *"Heil Hitler!"* as thousands of uniformed arms shot out in the Nazi salute. He told Inge that during the entire weeklong event, he did not hear a single "sensible conversation."

It didn't help when, after he returned, a Hitler Youth official asked to see the book he was reading on a camping trip. He handed the book over, a copy of *Sternstunden der Menschheit* (Mankind's Stellar Hours) by the Jewish writer Stefan Zweig. The Nazis had banned all of Zweig's books. Hans was told he should not be reading such "Jewish filth." His copy was confiscated.

Then he was reprimanded for singing Russian, Swedish, and Balkan folk songs as he sat with his boys around a campfire. Foreign songs were not allowed! Stick to German songs, he was told, especially officially approved Nazi songs. Hans laughed at this order, thinking it could not be meant seriously. When he argued that the boys in his squad were turned off by the endless singing of dreary Nazi songs, he was threatened with punishment.

Later he thought of a way to increase his boys' pride in their squad. He had them design and sew a distinctive flag of their own. They decorated it with a picture of a mythical beast, mounted it on a flagpole, and solemnly dedicated it to the Führer. It would fly alongside their Nazi swastika flag as a symbol of their special fellowship.

One evening as they stood in formation for review, a ranking Hitler Youth leader ordered the squad's twelve-year-old flag bearer to hand over the new flag. "You don't need a banner of your own," he said. "Use the [Nazi flag] prescribed for everyone."

The boy hesitated. He stood rigidly at attention, uncertain how to respond. "Hand it over!" barked the leader. When he repeated the order a third time in a threatening voice, Hans stepped out of the ranks. "Let him keep the flag," he protested. "Stop bullying him."

"You have no right to make a flag of your own," the leader shouted. "You are to stick strictly to the flags prescribed in the manuals."

Hans tried to explain that the flag meant a great deal to his boys. The leader ignored him and reached out to wrest the flag from the twelve-year-old's trembling hands. Hans pushed him away. They scuffled, and without thinking, Hans slapped the Hitler Youth leader.

That ended his career as a squad leader.

It was just as well. Lots of young people found the militaristic nature of the Hitler Youth distasteful. "We hardly had any free time," a former member recalled. "Everything was done in a military way. . . . The camp leader was an older Hitler Youth functionary of the drill sergeant type. His entire education effort was barking out orders."

Rifle practice at a Hitler Youth summer camp, 1941. The boys were taught to handle weapons, throw hand grenades, dig trenches and foxholes, and stalk, ambush, and kill enemies. A sign above the camp gate announced WE ARE BORN TO DIE FOR GERMANY.

Hans's distaste for military drill and regimentation had drawn him to an underground youth group known as d.j.1.11 — short for *Deutsche Jungendschaft* (German Boys' League) of 1 November (1929), the date the group was founded. When membership in the Hitler Youth became mandatory in 1936, the Nazis outlawed all other German youth groups. Most disbanded, but followers of the d.j.1.11 continued to meet secretly in cities across Germany.

Soon after joining the Hitler Youth, Hans, together with some friends, formed an independent branch of the d.j.1.11. "Our communal excursions and evening get-togethers helped us acquire [an inner] strength," Hans told his parents, "and we'll never, ever forget those trips. We certainly had a boyhood worthy of the name!"

Like the Hitler Youth, members of the underground group went on hikes and camping trips. But they did not march, salute, or wear uniforms. They dressed as they pleased and spoke with secret code words and phrases that outsiders would not understand. They read forbidden books, sang songs from around the world, ran wildly through the woods, and plunged into icy streams before breakfast. And they poked fun at self-important Nazi officials and traded jokes about Hitler that could have landed them in prison.

"What is an Aryan?" one boy would ask.

The group would reply in hooting unison: "Blond like Hitler!" — who was dark. "Tall like Goebbels!" — the propaganda minister, who was short. "Slender like Göring!" — the Nazi military leader, who was fat.

Propaganda minister Josef Goebbels (*left*) and military leader Hermann Göring, along with other high-ranking Nazis, were the butt of forbidden jokes told by members of the outlawed youth group d.j.1.11.

A group from the *Bund Deutscher Madel* (League of German Girls) on an outing. Sophie Scholl enjoyed the hiking and camping, but, like her brother, Hans, became disillusioned.

By now, the rumblings of doubt that had turned Hans away from the Hitler Youth had spread to others in his family. At first, Sophie had found in the League of German Girls an outlet for her love of nature. She enjoyed the hikes and camping, the music and fellowship. She too was appointed a squad leader. But Sophie, "the wisest of my women," as her father called her, was not easily fooled, and she began to share the discontent that had led Hans down a different path.

Nazi storm troopers link hands at the entrance to the University of Vienna, preventing Jews from entering the building, 1938. Under the Nuremberg Laws, German Jews were barred from schools, parks, swimming pools, concert halls, and public transportation.

Sophie was remembered by a childhood friend as being "very serious and yet very fun-loving." She loved to dance. "She danced with great abandon," Inge recalled. "She let the music carry her away, oblivious to her surroundings, truly going along with her partner." By turns joyous and thoughtful, she would often retire quietly to a private world of her own.

Like Hans, Sophie was caught reading a banned book — a collection of songs by the renowned German poet Heinrich Heine, who happened to be Jewish. The Nazis had outlawed all of Heine's works. When Sophie was warned not to read "degenerate" Jewish books, which had been banned and burned, she stubbornly replied, "He who doesn't know Heinrich Heine doesn't know German literature." In fact, a century earlier, Heine had warned with tremendous foresight, "Where one burns books, one will, in the end, burn people."

Two Jewish girls, Anneliese Wallersteiner and Luise Nathan, were classmates and close friends of Sophie's. She was enraged when they were not allowed to join the League of German Girls. "Why can't Luise, with her fair hair and blue eyes, be a member, while I with my dark hair and dark eyes am a member?" she asked.

Germany's half million Jews — one percent of the population — were about to become outcasts. With the introduction of the Nuremberg Race Laws in September 1935, they were stripped of their German citizenship. The Jewish girls in Sophie's class, along with Jewish students across the country, were sent to separate schools and barred from movie theaters, swimming pools, sports centers, and parks. Germans who maintained open friendships with Jews now came under suspicion. Even so, Sophie insisted on continuing her friendship with Anneliese and Luise. "She just could not understand, much less accept, anti-Jewish racism," said Inge.

Rumors were circulating about political opponents of the Nazis being hauled off to concentration camps, where prisoners were confined under harsh and often brutal conditions. "Father, what is a concentration camp?" Inge asked at dinner one evening. Robert Scholl told his children what he knew and what he suspected. "Why are those who are released from them forbidden on pain of death to tell anything about what they went through?" he wondered.

One day a popular Ulm schoolteacher disappeared and wasn't heard from again. People assumed he had been sent to a concentration camp.

Hans Scholl served his required six-month stint with the Reich Labor Service living and working with a road-building crew.

"What did he do?" the Scholls asked the teacher's mother. "Nothing. Nothing," she replied in despair. "He just wasn't a Nazi, it was impossible for him to belong." She added, "*That* was his crime."

"There awoke in us a feeling of living in a house once beautiful and clean but in whose cellars behind locked doors frightful, evil, and fearsome things were happening," Inge wrote. "Doubt had slowly taken hold of us."

The Scholl apartment on Cathedral Square became a gathering place for a secret reading circle that met in private homes to discuss forbidden books. "We have a large circle — all of them anti-Hitler," one participant told Inge. "And each of these friends has his own separate circle which is anti-Hitler, and so on and so forth: a great underground network against Hitler. If only someone could get them to act collectively."

"In the home or with the family you could talk openly," Elisabeth Scholl recalled, "but outside the home you had to be very careful about making any critical comments about the regime, because you did not know whether a person was a Nazi or not."

In 1937, Hans graduated from high school with plans to study medicine at Munich University. Before entering college, he was required to serve six months in the National Labor Service, followed by two years of compulsory military service. He spent his labor assignment working and living with a road-building crew. "This place is a mine of experience," he wrote to his mother. "I'm putting my heart and soul into my work, believe me — I never shirk. The main external changes in me are shorter hair, a heavy tan, and a more relaxed expression."

After finishing his labor service, Hans was drafted. A keen horseman since boyhood, he applied to join a German army cavalry unit stationed at nearby Stuttgart. While he was undergoing basic training in the autumn of 1937, he learned that the Gestapo — the Nazi secret police — had arrested his brother, Werner, fifteen at the time, and his sisters Inge and Sophie.

Prisoners march around the courtyard of the Gestapo headquarters in Nuremberg.

* * * * THREE * * * *

HALF SOLDIER, HALF STUDENT

IN the autumn of 1937, the Gestapo began a sweeping crackdown on members of the banned youth group d.j.1.11 and its sympathizers. All over Germany, young people were arrested and taken to Gestapo headquarters in Stuttgart, among them Hans's brother, Werner, fifteen at the time, and his sisters Sophie and Inge. "My parents were shocked," Inge recalled. "They could not imagine that there were serious charges against us. . . . Each of us was put in a cell and no one knew what was going to happen."

Sophie was released later that day, but Werner, who had been active in Hans's d.j.1.11 group, and Inge, a devoted member of the League of German Girls, were held a week for questioning. After they were released, the Gestapo arrested Hans at his army barracks. He was driven to Gestapo headquarters in handcuffs, placed in solitary confinement, and subjected to weeks of interrogation. Because his activities in the d.j.1.11 had called attention to his family, he blamed himself for the arrests of his sisters and brother.

Following a visit from his father, Hans wrote to his parents from his cell at the detention prison: "Thank you so much for coming, Father. You brought me fresh hope. I'm so immensely sorry to have brought this misfortune on the family, and I was often close to despair during my first few days in detention. I promise you, though, I'll put everything right. When I'm free again, I'll work and work — that and nothing but — so you can look on your son with pride again."

The commanding officer of Hans's cavalry unit came to his aid, pressing for a speedy investigation. "Hans Scholl is ours," he told the Gestapo. "If there is something to be taken care of, we will take care of it." After five weeks, he managed to have Hans released. But Hans remained under investigation, charged with "subversive activities" for his role in the d.j.1.11.

The Gestapo also accused Hans of having had a gay sexual relationship — a criminal offense in Nazi Germany — with another teenage boy when they were members of the Hitler Youth. Under questioning, Hans confessed to "a close relationship" with the boy. "I'm not afraid of going on trial," he wrote to his parents. "Even if I can't justify myself in open court, I can justify myself to myself."

He made a favorable impression on Judge Hermann Cuhorst, who heard his case. The judge criticized Hans for continuing to lead a group of friends whose activities had been banned, but explained his behavior as the "youthful exuberance" and "obstinate personality" of "a headstrong young man." The gay relationship, which was mutual, was passed off as a youthful "failing." All charges against Hans were dismissed. He was free to leave the courtroom with a clean record.

Even so, Hans was deeply shaken by what he felt was his unjustified imprisonment and by the intrusive interrogations probing his personal life. "I often forget the whole thing," he told Inge, "and act carefree and exuberant. But then the dark shadow looms up again and makes everything seem dismal and empty. When that happens, all that keeps me going is the thought of a future that'll be better than the present. You've no idea how much I look forward to going to university."

The arrests had a profound and lasting effect

German pedestrians walk past the shattered windows of a Jewish-owned shop that was attacked on *Kristallnacht,* November 10, 1938.

on the entire Scholl family, deepening their alienation from the Nazi regime. Sophie felt that the charges against Hans were "totally unjustified." She resented her brother's treatment at the hands of the Gestapo, and claimed later that Hans's ordeal was an important motivation for her resistance activities.

Robert Scholl was furious. On a walk one evening with Sophie and Inge, he could not contain his rage. "If those bastards harm my children in any way," he exploded, "I'll go to Berlin and shoot him"— meaning Hitler.

* * *

Nazi persecution of the Jews, meanwhile, spilled into the streets with outbursts of violence. Nazi Germany, wrote the American reporter William Shirer, "had deliberately turned down a dark and savage road from which there was to be no return."

On the night of November 9, 1938, rampaging

This Sudeten woman cannot conceal her grief as she dutifully salutes triumphant German troops after Hitler's takeover of the Sudetenland, 1938. The Nazi salute was required by law.

mobs, spurred on by Nazi storm troopers, smashed the windows of Jewish shops and homes and set fire to hundreds of synagogues in cities and towns across Germany, while the police looked away. Thousands of Jews were herded into the streets, beaten, spat upon, and hauled off to concentration camps to be held in "protective custody." The night was called *Kristallnacht* (Night of Broken Glass) because the streets were littered with glass from shattered windows.

Many Germans were shocked by the brutality of the attacks. Some turned their faces away from the wreckage and wept. But the iron grip of the Nazi regime stifled any meaningful opposition. One newspaper ridiculed the "softhearted squeamishness" of those who expressed sympathy for Jewish victims of the violence. Most Germans kept their opinions to themselves. "The cowed middle classes stared at the Nazi monster like a rabbit at a snake," wrote one German observer.

When Hans completed his basic military training at Stuttgart, he was granted permission to study medicine while continuing his military service as a member of the

Victorious German troops parade through Warsaw, Poland, September 1939. Hitler's surprise invasion of Poland was the first step in his secret plan to dominate Europe.

army medical corps. In the spring of 1939, he enrolled as a full-time medical student at Munich University and was assigned to the local military hospital. "It was an unusual kind of life—half soldier, half student, sometimes in the barracks, at other times at the university or the hospital," Inge wrote.

Hans quickly formed friendships with several of his fellow student-soldiers, members of the army medical corps. They were drawn together by their shared enthusiasm for books and music and by their opposition to the Nazi regime, which they dared discuss only among themselves. While they were assigned to an army barracks, they were free to attend classes and rent student living quarters near the campus. Sophie, still in secondary school, looked forward to joining Hans and his friends at the university.

By now, Germany had renounced the Treaty of Versailles and restored its military might. The

Nazi government had annexed Austria, then the Sudetenland region of Czechoslovakia, and finally the rest of Czechoslovakia. As Hitler secretly planned for war in the summer of 1939, the Gestapo clamped down on all signs of dissent. "No one was secure against arrest," Inge Scholl wrote later. "One might be arrested in the street, because of some trivial remark, and disappear, perhaps forever. . . . All of Germany was spied upon, and secret ears listened everywhere."

That summer, Werner, seventeen at the time, became the first member of the Scholl family to engage in a public act of opposition to the Nazi regime. Late one night, he went to the Ulm courthouse, climbed to the top of the statue of Justice, and placed a blindfold marked with a swastika across the statue's eyes — a daring, even reckless, act that he did not admit to until many years later.

* * *

World War II began at dawn on September 1, 1939, when German troops marched into Poland. Two days later, France and Britain declared war on Germany, but it was too late to save the Poles. Overwhelmed by the Nazi Blitzkrieg, or "lightning war," Poland surrendered within a month.

"You and your men must have plenty to do now," Sophie wrote to her boyfriend, Fritz Hartnagel, an officer in the Signal Corps. "I just can't grasp that people's lives are now under constant threat from other people. I'll never understand it, and I find it terrible. Don't go telling me it's for the Fatherland's sake."

Hitler had vowed to dominate Europe by force. "Close your hearts to pity!" he told his generals. "Be steeled against all signs of compassion!"

His campaign on the western front was launched in April 1940, when German troops overran Denmark, Norway, Holland, and Belgium and invaded France. The British army was driven off the continent and into the sea at Dunkirk. By June, when France surrendered, all of Europe outside Britain was either an ally or satellite of Germany, or neutral. Hitler rode into occupied Paris and danced a victory jig in front of the Arch of Triumph.

Hans had to suspend his studies when his medical unit was assigned to an operating theater in Saint-Quentin, France. "We've commandeered the best available houses," he told his parents. "Personally, I felt more at home [sleeping] in the straw. What am I, a thief or a self-respecting

Adolf Hitler poses for a snapshot in Nazi-occupied Paris, June 23, 1940.

human being? You've no idea the looting that goes on." By summer's end, he was back at Munich University, attending classes again.

When Sophie graduated from high school, she planned to study philosophy and biology at Munich University. But before entering college, she was required to spend six months working for the State Labor Service. To get around that requirement, she enrolled in a practical course in kindergarten teaching. The teaching, she hoped,

Like these young women carrying pitchforks, Sophie Scholl served her required stint with the State Labor Service assigned to farm work.

would be an acceptable substitute for her labor service.

"The children give me a great deal of pleasure," she wrote to Fritz Hartnagel. "Working with them is an immensely tiring business, because you have to adjust to them completely. This certainly isn't an egotistical profession, and I doubt I could stick it indefinitely — I've been brought up too self-centered."

After working with children for almost a year, Sophie learned that the rules had changed and she still had to serve six months with the Labor Service. She was sent to a work camp in a rural area, where she lived in a dormitory with ten other uniformed girls and was assigned to jobs on local farms. Then she was informed that her compulsory labor service would be extended for an additional six months. This time she was sent to work as a kindergarten teacher at a nursery school in a small town near the Swiss border. Once again, her dream of studying at the university had to be put on hold.

"I doubt if my fury at the [extended service] will have subsided by Saturday," she wrote to Hans. "I'll be an old crone before I can start university — but I won't abandon the struggle in a hurry. I'd sooner take poison."

Finally, in May 1942, her compulsory service to the state behind her, Sophie was able to join her brother in Munich and begin her university studies. She was about to celebrate her twenty-first birthday.

Willi Graf.

FOUR

LEAFLETS OF THE WHITE ROSE

IT seems almost unbelievable that I'll be able to start at the university tomorrow," Sophie told her mother. Simply gaining admission was in itself an accomplishment. At the time, the quota for female students at German universities was set at just 10 percent of the student body.

Inge saw Sophie off at the Ulm train station. "I can still see her as she stood before me . . . ready to start and full of expectation," Inge recalled. Sophie was wearing a daisy behind her ear. Packed carefully in her handbag was a "crisp, brown, sweet-smelling cake" her mother had baked, and next to it a bottle of wine for her birthday celebration that evening.

Hans and his girlfriend at the time, Traute Lafrenz, a medical student from Hamburg, were waiting to greet Sophie as her train pulled

Hans Scholl as a medical student at Munich University (*left*).

Sophie Scholl as a philosophy and biology student (*right*).

into the Munich station. "Tonight you'll meet my friends," he told her. They gathered that evening at Hans's room near the campus. Prints of French Impressionist paintings (condemned by the Nazis as "degenerate art") were pinned to the walls, and books were scattered about everywhere. Among the guests, as Inge reported later, were three of Hans's closest university friends, all medical students and members of the army medical corps — Alexander Schmorell, Christoph Probst, and Willi Graf.

Alex, tall and witty, a lover of practical jokes, had been born in Russia and brought to Germany as a child. His mother was Russian, his father a prominent Munich physician. Raised by a Russian nanny, Alex spoke Russian fluently and loved to sing Russian folk songs.

Willi, thoughtful and reserved, was the quiet one. "When he says anything, in his very deliberate way," Sophie observed, "one has the impression that he would not speak unless he could commit himself with his whole being." Raised in a devout Roman Catholic household, Willi had refused to join the Hitler Youth. Like Hans, he had been arrested by the Gestapo and jailed for his involvement with an outlawed youth group.

Christoph, alone among the students, was married. He had two small sons and a third child on the way. His stepmother was Jewish, and while growing up he had had many Jewish friends. "He was deeply upset," a friend recalled, "about the yellow star the Jews were forced to wear . . . [and by] reports coming in of mass atrocities at concentration camps."

It was a beautiful May evening, so they decided to take Sophie's bottle of wine to the English Garden, an inviting park near the campus. They tied a string to the bottle and immersed it in the stream that flowed through the park. Alex had brought his Russian balalaika and Hans his guitar, and as the wine cooled and the moon rose over Munich, they began to play and sing as Willi whistled through his fingers. "All at once they were singing happily and wildly, like persons under a spell," Inge wrote later.

Sophie rented a room of her own and became part of Hans's inner circle. They met often, joined by like-minded friends, at cafés, in Hans's room, at the home of Alex's parents. "They would recommend books to one another, read aloud, and hold discussions," Inge wrote, "but sometimes they would suddenly be seized by wild high

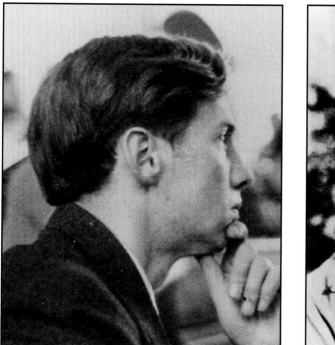

Alexander Schmorell (*left*).

Christoph Probst (*right*).

Students on their way to class at Munich University.

spirits and invent all sorts of nonsense. Their excess of imagination, humor, and love of life had to be given vent from time to time."

More and more often, their discussions turned to Nazi repression at home and, as German forces overran Poland and launched a surprise invasion of the Soviet Union, to crimes being committed against people in the occupied territories. They asked themselves: How should a responsible citizen act under a dictatorship? How could they resist the Nazi regime? But it was dangerous to speak openly in public. "You had to keep everything secret," recalled George Wittenstein, a fellow medical student who often joined the group. "You could not even trust your friends. . . . It would be weeks and months before you knew someone well enough that you could talk to them."

They heard rumors of death camps in Poland, of the mass murder of Jews in the Soviet Union. Their Jewish friends and neighbors were disappearing. It was difficult to know exactly what was going on, because the Nazi Ministry of Propaganda censored newspapers and the radio. It was a crime to listen to foreign radio broadcasts.

But the increasingly alarming reports could not be silenced. The Catholic bishop of Munster, Clemens August Graf von Galen, had delivered a scathing sermon denouncing the Nazis' top-secret euthanasia program — the systematic killing, by means of lethal gas, of mental patients and physically handicapped adults and children. The official policy, said Galen, made it "permissible to destroy 'life which does not deserve to live'— to kill innocent persons, if it is decided

A Jewish merchant and his daughter, friends of the Scholl family, cross the Stuttgarter Strasse bridge in Ulm, passing a sign that reads: JEWS ARE NOT DESIRABLE IN ULM! 1937.

that such lives are no longer of value to [the German people].

"It is a terrible doctrine," the bishop declared, "which excuses the murder of innocent people, which gives express license to kill unemployable invalids, cripples, incurables, and the seniles and those who suffer from incurable disease."

The Roman Catholic bishop Clemens A. Graf von Galen. He denounced the Nazis' top-secret euthanasia program as a "terrible doctrine" designed to "kill innocent people."

Copies of Bishop Galen's sermon had been run off on a mimeograph machine and mailed to people believed to be sympathetic. The Scholls found a copy in their mailbox. "Finally a man has had the courage to speak out," Hans exclaimed after reading the sermon. He studied the pages he was holding, then added, "We really ought to have a duplicating machine."

Hans had been examining his conscience. He felt compelled by his times to embark on an inner journey of discovery. Though a medical student, he read classic German authors and philosophers such as Goethe and Schilling, as well as the Greek philosopher Aristotle and the ancient Chinese book of wisdom, the *Tao Te Ching*. And he studied passages in the Bible that now took on new meanings. "What I seek is purification. I want all the shadows to melt away from me," he confided to his diary. "I'm searching for myself, just myself, because this much I do know: I'll only find the truth inside me."

Sophie, too, was seeking guidance in her reading, in conversation, and in prayer. "There's something new for me to digest here every day," she wrote to a friend. "I've an urge to act on what has so far existed within me merely as an idea — as what I perceive to be right."

Hartheim Castle, one of six Nazi euthanasia killing centers where people deemed "unworthy of life" because of physical or mental disabilities were killed by lethal injection or by gassing.

One evening, Hans and some friends were discussing their work in the hospitals and clinics. "There's nothing more pleasant than going from bed to bed and having the sense of holding in your hands a life in peril," Hans said. "There are moments when I'm absolutely happy."

"But isn't it preposterous," one of his friends interrupted, "that we sit in our rooms and study how to heal mankind when on the outside the state every day sends countless young people to their death? What in the world are we waiting for? Until one day the war is over and all nations point to us and say that we accepted this government without resisting?"

✳ ✳ ✳

Copies of the first anti-Nazi leaflet appeared in Munich mailboxes at the end of June 1942. The heading read: "Leaflets of the White Rose."

The Nazis used mobile gas vans like this one to exterminate disabled patients. The victims were locked in an airtight compartment into which exhaust fumes were piped while the van's engine was running, resulting in death by carbon monoxide poisoning. The vans were the forerunners of concentration camp gas chambers disguised as shower rooms, in which millions died.

"Is it not true that every honest German today is ashamed of his government?" the leaflet demanded. "Therefore, every individual must be aware of his responsibility as a member of western culture and put up as fierce a fight as possible; he must work against the scourges of mankind, against fascism and any similar system of totalitarianism.

"Offer resistance—*resistance*—wherever you may be . . . before it is too late; before the last city, like Cologne, lies in ruins; and before the nation's last young man has bled to death somewhere on the battlefields for the hubris of a subhuman."

The leaflet ends by invoking the figure of Hope, in a play by Goethe, who proclaims:

> Now I find my good men
> Are gathered in the night,
> To wait in silence, not to sleep.
> And the glorious word of liberty
> They whisper and murmur,
> Till in unaccustomed strangeness,
> On the steps of our temple
> Once again in delight they cry:
> Freedom! Freedom! Freedom!

The leaflet, a collaboration between Hans and Alex, had been typed on a borrowed portable typewriter and copied on a mimeograph machine Hans had bought at a local office supply shop. Just one hundred copies had been mailed to addresses taken from the Munich phone directory — to persons believed to be sympathetic and to a few beer hall owners in hopes they would pass the leaflets on to their customers. "Please make as many copies of this leaflet as you can and distribute them," the leaflet requested.

"The name [White Rose] was chosen arbitrarily," Hans claimed later. "I proceeded from the assumption that powerful propaganda has to contain certain phrases which do not necessarily mean anything but sound good and give the impression of a political program." He may also have had in mind that a white rose is a symbol of purity and innocence.

At first only Hans, Alex, Willi Graf, and Christoph Probst knew who had written the leaflet. They were keenly aware that any form of opposition to the Nazis carried the risk of death, so they did not tell Sophie or their other friends about their plans. When Traute Lafrenz saw a copy, she recalled, "I could tell at once that it must have been written by 'us,' though I still wasn't sure that Hans himself had done it."

Sophie had been at the university about six weeks when the leaflet appeared. Hans tried to evade her questions about it. "It's not a good idea to ask who wrote the leaflet," he told her, "as that person's life might be endangered." But Sophie

Flugblätter der Weissen Rose.

I

Nichts ist eines Kulturvolkes unwürdiger, als sich ohne Widerstand von einer verantwortungslosen und dunklen Trieben ergebenen Herrscherclique "regieren" zu lassen. Ist es nicht so, dass sich jeder ehrliche Deutsche heute seiner Regierung schämt, und wer von uns ahnt das Ausmass der Schmach, die über uns und unsere Kinder kommen wird, wenn einst der Schleier von unseren Augen gefallen ist und die grauenvollsten und jegliches Mass unendlich überschreitenden Verbrechen ans Tageslicht treten? Wenn das deutsche Volk schon so in seinem tiefsten Wesen korrumpiert und zerfallen ist, dass es ohne eine Hand zu regen, im leichtsinnigen Vertrauen auf eine fragwürdige Gesetzmässigkeit der Geschichte, das Höchste, das ein Mensch besitzt, und das ihn über jede andere Kreatur erhöht, nämlich den freien Willen, preisgibt, die Freiheit des Menschen preisgibt, selbst mit einzugreifen in das Rad der Geschichte und es seiner vernünftigen Entscheidung unterzuordnen, wenn die Deutschen so jeder Individualität bar, schon so sehr zur geistlosen und feigen Masse geworden sind, dann, ja dann verdienen sie den Untergang.

Goethe spricht von den Deutschen als einem tragischen Volke, gleich dem der Juden und Griechen, aber heute hat es eher den Anschein, als sei es eine seichte, willenlose Herde von Mitläufern, denen das Mark aus dem Innersten gesogen und nun ihres Kernes beraubt, bereit sind sich in den Untergang hetzen zu lassen. Es scheint so - aber es ist nicht so; vielmehr hat man in langsamer, trügerischer, systematischer Vergewaltigung jeden einzelnen in ein geistiges Gefängnis gesteckt, und erst, als er darin gefesselt lag, wurde er sich des Verhängnisses bewusst. Wenige nur erkannten das drohende Verderben, und der Lohn für ihr heroisches Mahnen war der Tod. Ueber das Schicksal dieser Menschen wird noch zu reden sein.

Wenn jeder wartet, bis der Andere anfängt, werden die Boten der rächenden Nemesis unaufhaltsam näher und näher rücken, dann wird auch das letzte Opfer sinnlos in den Rachen des unersättlichen Dämons geworfen sein. Daher muss jeder Einzelne seiner Verantwortung als Mitglied der christlichen und abendländischen Kultur bewusst in dieser letzten Stunde sich wehren so viel er kann, arbeiten wider die Geisel der Menschheit, wider den Faschismus und jedes ihm ähnliche System des absoluten Staates. Leistet passiven Widerstand - W i d e r s t a n d - wo immer Ihr auch seid, verhindert das Weiterlaufen dieser atheistischen Kriegsmaschine, ehe es zu spät ist, ehe die letzten Städte ein Trümmerhaufen sind, gleich Köln, und ehe die letzte Jugend des Volkes irgendwo für die Hybris eines Untermenschen verblutet ist. Vergesst nicht, dass ein jedes Volk diejenige Regierung verdient, die es erträgt!

Aus Friedrich Schiller, "Die Gesetzgebung des Lykurgus und Solon":

"....Gegen seinen eigenen Zweck gehalten, ist die Gesetzgebung des Lykurgus ein Meisterstück der Staats- und Menschenkunde. Er wollte einen mächtigen, in sich selbst gegründeten, unzerstörbaren Staat; politische Stärke und Dauerhaftigkeit waren das Ziel, wonach er strebte, und dieses Ziel hat er so weit erreicht, als unter seinen Umständen möglich war, Aber hält man den Zweck, welchen Lykurgus sich vorsetzte, gegen den Zweck der Menschheit, so muss eine tiefe Missbilligung an die Stelle der Bewunderung treten, die uns der erste, flüchtige Blick abgewonnen hat. Alles darf dem Besten des Staates zum Opfer gebracht werden, nur dasjenige nicht, dem der Staat selbst nur als ein Mittel dient, Der Staat selbst ist niemals Zweck, er ist nur wichtig als eine Bedingung, unter welcher der Zweck der Menschheit erfüllt werden kann, und dieser Zweck der Menschheit ist kein anderer, als Ausbildung aller Kräfte des Menschen, Fort-

---

Leaflets of the White Rose

I

Nothing is more dishonourable for a civilized people than to let itself be "governed" without resistance by an irresponsible clique of rulers devoted to dark instincts. Is it not true that every honest German today is ashamed of his government? And who among us can sense the dimensions of the dishonor that will lie upon us and our children once the veil has fallen from our eyes and the most horrid and extravagant crimes come to light? If German people are already so corrupted and spiritually crushed that they do not raise a hand, frivolously trusting in a questionable faith in the lawful order of history; if they surrender man's highest principle, that which raises him above all other God's creatures, his free will; if they abandon the determination to take decisive action and turn the wheel of history and thus subject it to their own rational decision; if they are so devoid of all individuality, have already gone so far along the road to turning into a spiritless and cowardly mass – then they clearly deserve their downfall.

Goethe speaks of the Germans as a tragic people, similar to the Jews or the Greeks, but today it would appear rather as a shallow, spineless herd of followers robbed of their core with the marrow sucked out of them, who are now just waiting to be hounded to their destruction. So it seems – but it is not so. Through gradual, treacherous, systematic violation, every single person has rather been put into a prison of the mind, which he only realizes after finding himself already in chains. Only a few have recognized the impending doom and their heroic warnings have been rewarded with death. The fate of these persons will be spoken of later.

If everyone waits for his neighbour to take the first step, the messengers of the vengeful nemesis will come ever closer, and the very last victim will senselessly be thrown into the throat of the insatiable demon. Therefore, every individual must be aware of his responsibility as a member of western culture and put up as fierce a fight as possible, he must work against the scourges of mankind, against fascism and any similar system of totalitarianism. Offer resistance – *resistance* – wherever you may be, stop this atheistic war machine from running on and on, before it is too late; before the last city, like Cologne, lies in ruins; and before the nation's last young man has bled to death somewhere on the battlefields for the hubris of a subhuman. Don't forget that every people deserves the regime it is willing to endure!

Excerpt from Friedrich Schiller's The Legislation of Lycurgus and Solon:

"...Viewed in relation to its purpose, the legal code of Lycurgus is a masterpiece of political science and knowledge of human nature. He desired a powerful, indestructible state, firmly established on its own principles. His goal was to achieve political power and permanence, and he attained this goal to the fullest extent possible under the circumstances. But if one compares Lycurgus' purpose with those of mankind, then a deep disapproval must take the place of the admiration which we felt at first glance. Anything may be sacrificed for the good of the State except that end which the State itself only serves as a means. The State is never an end in itself; it is important only as a condition under which the purpose of mankind can be attained, and this purpose is no less than the development of all human resources, progress. If a political constitution prevents the development of the capabilities which reside in man, if it interferes with the progress of the human spirit, then it is reprehensible and injurious, no matter how excellently devised, how perfect in its own way. Its very permanence in that case amounts more to a reproach than to a basis for fame; it becomes a prolonged evil, and the longer it endures, the more harmful it is.

...At the cost of all moral feeling a political merit was achieved, and the resources of the state were mobilized to that end. In Sparta there was no conjugal love, no mother love, no filial love, no friendship; all men were citizens only, and all virtue was civic.

...It was the Spartans' duty by law to be inhumane to their slaves; with these unhappy victims of war humanity itself was insulted and mistreated. In the Spartan code of law the dangerous principle was

---

Partial facsimile and translation of the first White Rose leaflet.

persisted, and when Hans finally admitted that he and Alex were the authors, she insisted on becoming fully involved. "She knew that [Hans] had crossed the boundary within which people conduct their lives in safety and comfort," Inge wrote. "There was no way back."

The idea for the leaflet had not originated with any one person. It had evolved out of months of discussions and a growing sense of trust among a small circle of friends. All of them were repelled by what was happening in Germany. They yearned to speak freely, to be entirely themselves again. And all had been deeply influenced, each in his or her own way, by religious ideals.

The young men and women of the White Rose were ready to act, and they chose a nonviolent form of resistance to rally the conscience of the nation through printed words. "They could have chosen to throw bombs," Inge Scholl remarked years later.

Storm troopers guard a column of Polish Jews being
marched off to Nazi death camps, Warsaw, c. 1942.

FIVE

"WE ARE YOUR BAD CONSCIENCE"

THREE more White Rose leaflets were produced that summer in rapid succession. By the end of July, a dozen students were involved in the secret undertaking. Their leaflets attacking Hitler and the Nazis had appeared in several German cities.

A Munich architect, Manfred Eickemeyer, offered his secluded studio as a meeting place for the White Rose students. At considerable risk to himself, he allowed them to print leaflets and store their duplicating equipment in the cellar beneath the studio.

Working in the cellar at night, they cranked out thousands of leaflets on their hand-operated mimeograph machine. To avoid suspicion when they needed supplies, they would fan out across Munich and buy small amounts of paper, envelopes, stencils, and postage stamps at widely scattered shops and post offices — a ream of paper here, a box of envelopes there, never too much of anything at any one store.

Hans and Alex continued to write the leaflets, with feedback from other members of the group. Their first leaflet had called on German citizens to resist the Nazi regime. The second zeroed in on Nazi atrocities in the occupied territories.

Manfred Eickemeyer had recently returned from Nazi-occupied Poland. He had personally witnessed forced deportations of Jews and other despised groups and learned of mass executions carried out by special units of the German armed forces called *Einsatztruppen* (shock troops). He told Hans and Alex how these special-duty troops rounded up men, women, and children. They seized their valuables, herded them into trucks, and took them to the outskirts of town, where they were ordered to dig trenches. Lined up at the edge of the trenches, the victims were machine-gunned. They tumbled one after another into the graves they had dug for themselves.

Rumors about the mass killings had been circulating for some time, but most people could not

A woman pleads for mercy during the forced deportation of Polish Jews from the Warsaw ghetto, c. 1942.

High tech, circa 1942: With this hand-operated mimeograph machine, the Munich students cranked out thousands of White Rose leaflets.

bring themselves to believe such horror stories. Eickemeyer's anguished account was the first on-the-scene report Hans and Alex had heard. The architect wanted the world to know what he had witnessed.

"Since the conquest of Poland," the second White Rose leaflet reported, "<u>three hundred thousand</u> Jews have been murdered in this country in the most bestial way. Here we see the most frightful crime against human dignity, a crime that is unparalleled in the whole of history."

The leaflet continues, "Each [German] wants to be exonerated of a guilt of this kind, each one

continues on his way with the . . . calmest conscience. But he cannot be exonerated; he is guilty, guilty, guilty!"

The third leaflet assailed the Nazi "dictatorship of evil." While it emphasized passive resistance, it added, "In this struggle we must not recoil from any course, any action, whatever its nature." It called for "Sabotage in armament plants and war industries, sabotage at all gatherings, rallies, public ceremonies, and organizations of the National Socialist Party. . . . Sabotage in all the areas of science and scholarship which further the continuation of the war. . . . Sabotage in all branches of the arts. . . . Sabotage in all publications, all newspapers, that are in the pay of the 'government' and that defend its ideology."

The Führer himself was the target of the fourth leaflet: "Every word that comes from Hitler's mouth is a lie. When he says peace, he means war, and when he blasphemously uses the name of the Almighty, he means the power of evil, the fallen angel, Satan. His mouth is the foul-smelling maw of Hell, and his might is at bottom accursed."

This leaflet ended with the words "We will not be silent. We are your bad conscience. The White Rose will not leave you in peace!"

At the Munich train station, Sophie Scholl, sniffing a white rose, bids farewell to
Hans Scholl (far left), Willi Graf (back to camera), Alexander Schmorell (far right),
and their fellow student medics as they depart for the Russian war front, June 1942.

Hans Scholl and Alexander Schmorell relax aboard the troop train taking them to the Russian war front.

As the leaflets appeared one after another in June and July of 1942, German armies were advancing deep into the Soviet Union. When the summer semester ended, Hans and some of his fellow medical students were sent to the Russian front to serve as medics. Sophie saw them off at the Munich train station. "Hans went off to Russia last week with all the other people I've made friends with over the past few weeks and months," she told a friend. "I still preserve such a

Hans Scholl, Willi Graf, and Alexander Schmorell (*second, third, and fourth from left*) share a meal with fellow medics at their army base in Russia, summer 1942.

vivid recollection of every little farewell word and gesture. I'd never have believed I could become so attached to them all."

After a three-day train trip across Germany and Poland, the group reached Warsaw, already a war-ravaged city. Jews from all over the occupied territories had been herded behind the walls and barbed wire of the Warsaw Ghetto. By the time Hans and his friends arrived, most of the Jewish population, men, women, and children, had been marched from the ghetto through the streets of Warsaw to the train station, packed into sealed cattle cars, and shipped to Auschwitz and other death camps. Most of those remaining in the ghetto had been wiped out by starvation and epidemics. "The misery stares us in the face," Willi Graf wrote in his journal. "I hope I never see Warsaw in these conditions again." In a letter to Kurt Huber, one of his professors, Hans wrote, "The city, the [Jewish] Ghetto, the whole setup made a profound impression on all of us."

As their train approached the Russian war front, Hans marveled at the unending sweep of the Russian steppes. "Russia is so vast," he told Kurt Huber, "so boundless in every respect, and its inhabitants' love of their natural land is boundless too."

Hitler had set his sights on this vast and fertile expanse of territory as the place to establish *Lebensraum,* "living space," for the German people. Nazi propaganda had declared that the Slavic peoples, Russians among them, were "Asiatic inferiors," destined to be swept away and replaced by the Aryan master race. "This struggle," said Hitler, "is one of . . . racial differences and will have to be conducted with . . . unmerciful and relentless harshness."

Hans and his friends were assigned to a field hospital several miles from the front. Because Alex spoke Russian, he was able to take the group into the homes of local peasants, bringing wine and medicine as peace offerings and extending his hand in friendship. He asked the peasants to sing their folk songs for the smiling young visitors standing awkwardly by in their dusty gray enemy uniforms, and he in turn played his balalaika and sang German folk songs. These meetings, strictly forbidden by the German military, took place in the evenings at homes a safe distance from the German base.

"We have often eaten and sung with the peasants and had them play their wonderful melodies for us," Willi wrote. "Sometimes one is able to forget for a while all the sad and terrible things happening around us."

Hans felt himself "ripped apart," tending the wounded and dying by day as guns thundered nearby, then singing and dancing by night: "In the evening we listen to Russian songs at a woman's house. . . . We sit in the open air, behind the trees, the moon comes up, its rays falling in the spaces between the rows of trees, it's cool, the girls sing to the guitar, we try to hum the bass part, it's so beautiful, you feel Russia's heart, we love it."

By chance, Hans's brother, Werner, was

assigned to same sector of the Russian front. He was stationed just a few miles away. Borrowing a horse from his cavalry unit, Hans was able to ride over to see Werner from time to time. "We went for a long walk together and wound up at a Russian farmhouse . . . and sang Russian songs as though we were in the depths of peacetime," he told his parents.

That autumn, Hans and Werner learned that their father had been imprisoned. The Gestapo had arrested Robert Scholl after his secretary had denounced him for an offhand remark made in his office. In an unguarded moment, he had called Hitler "God's scourge on mankind," adding, "If the war doesn't end soon the Russians will be sitting in Berlin in two years." A Nazi court convicted him of "malicious slander of the Führer." He was sentenced to four months in prison and banned from practicing law because he was "politically unreliable."

"Even though I wasn't surprised by the [verdict], I didn't take it calmly," Hans wrote to his mother. "Indignation and turmoil filled my heart when I read your letter, and it took me a while to calm down again. . . . Father is in for a very hard time at first, as I know too well: starved of contact with the outside world, cooped up alone in a cramped gray cell."

At the end of October, Hans's medical group ended its tour of duty and was sent back to Germany to begin the winter semester at Munich

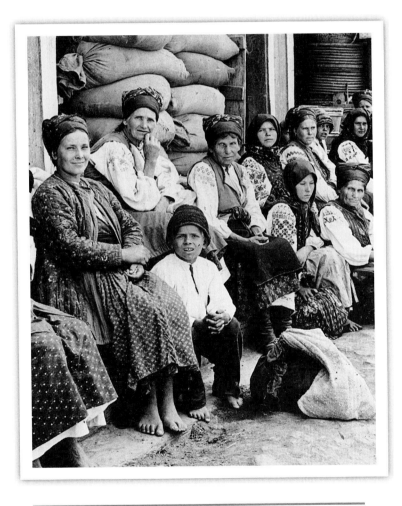

Russian peasants. Speaking fluent Russian, Alexander Schmorell defied army regulations by taking his fellow medics into the homes of local people.

On the last day of their service in Russia, Hans Scholl, Willi Graf, and Alexander Schmorell posed for this farewell photo with fellow medics from the 252nd Infantry Division, November 1942. Individuals are not identified.

University. "I marvel anew every day at the beauty of Russia," Hans wrote to his parents as he got ready to leave. "I think I'll often be overcome with nostalgia for this place when I'm back in Germany."

He was already planning the next phase of the White Rose leaflet campaign.

While couriers were dropping White Rose leaflets into mailboxes across the south of Germany, British and American warplanes were dropping blockbuster bombs on German cities and industrial sites. This aerial view shows an American Eighth Air Force bomber that has just raided an aircraft plant in Marienburg, Germany, 1943.

✳ ✳ ✳ ✳ SIX ✳ ✳ ✳ ✳

"DOWN WITH HITLER!"

WHILE Hans was in Russia, Sophie was working at a munitions factory in Ulm. Along with her university studies, she was required to devote two months each summer to war service work.

All her fellow workers were women, and most of them were forced laborers conscripted in Russia by the invading German army. The Russians lived in a barracks behind barbed wire, received a daily ration of watery soup, and worked seventy hours a week. The German women worked sixty hours, "standing over a machine and going through the same motions all day long. The sight of so many people in front of so many machines is depressing," Sophie told a friend.

Sophie made friends with a "delightful" Russian woman working at the machine next to her. They communicated by sign language and smiles. "I do my best to correct her picture of the German people," Sophie told a friend, "but a lot of the German women are also friendly and helpful to her, surprised to find that even Russians can be human beings."

Sophie's father was serving his sentence that summer at a prison nearby. After work in the evening she would go over to the prison grounds with her flute, stand outside the wall as close as possible to the barred windows, and play a melody her father loved: "Thoughts Are Free."

Thoughts are free,
Who can guess them?
They fly by
Like nocturnal shadows.
No man can know them,
No hunter can shoot them
With powder and lead.
Thoughts are free!

Hans and his companions returned from the Russian front that autumn and joined Sophie at the university. Once again they resumed their lives as students. They attended classroom lectures, went to concerts, sang in the Bach choir, and met for evening readings and discussions at private homes. At the same time, secretly and cautiously, they were expanding their circle of helpers and forging links with resistance groups in other German cities.

Hans's girlfriend, Traute, obtained a larger

Kurt Huber, professor of philosophy at Munich University. He insisted on writing the sixth White Rose leaflet.

mimeograph machine from her uncle's office supply store. When she went home to Hamburg for Christmas, she took along some White Rose leaflets and showed them to friends at Hamburg University. They offered to reproduce the leaflets and circulate them in their area. They became known as the Hamburg branch of the White Rose.

Willi Graf recruited friends to reproduce leaflets in his hometown of Saarbrücken. Hans and Alex were put in touch with an undercover resistance group that was working from within the Nazi government in Berlin. In Ulm, Sophie persuaded two school friends, Hans Hirzel and Franz Müller, to join the leaflet campaign. Working secretly behind the organ at the Martin Luther Church, where Hirzel's father (who knew nothing about this) was the pastor, Hirzel and Müller printed hundreds of leaflets and mailed them to other German cities.

These activities were carried out at great risk and with the utmost secrecy. "No family knew. Not one," Franz Müller recalled. "It was always in the back of our minds that they could arrest our families."

Sophie and Hans were both feeling the tension. "I'm never free for a moment from the depressing . . . state of uncertainty in which we live these days," Sophie confided to a friend. "Every word has to be examined from every angle before it is uttered." And Hans told a friend of his, "Life has become an ever-present danger."

Hans and Alex decided to approach Kurt Huber, the popular professor of philosophy Hans had written to while in Russia. Huber, they believed, was sympathetic to their views. His witty and challenging lectures, held at the university's largest lecture hall, attracted capacity crowds of students.

Hans and Alex called on Huber at his home in Munich. They told him about the growing network of resistance groups they had contacted, and about their plans to circulate new leaflets. Huber agreed to take part in their campaign. Forty-nine years old, a family man with graying hair and a slight limp, he was twice the age of the student activists who invited him into their secret circle.

The group's next leaflet, the fifth, no longer carried the name of the White Rose. Instead, it was headed "Leaflets of the Resistance in Germany." Professor Huber read two drafts of the

Prisoners at forced labor in a German aircraft plant. Sophie Scholl was assigned for two summer months to an Ulm munitions factory, where she worked alongside Russian women forced laborers.

leaflet and suggested several changes before it was printed.

Titled "A Call to All Germans," the leaflet declared:

> The war is approaching its destined end. . . . In the East the armies are constantly in retreat and invasion is imminent in the West. Mobilization in the United States has not yet reached its climax, but already it exceeds anything that the world has ever seen. It has become a mathematical certainty that Hitler is leading the German people into the abyss. <u>Hitler cannot win the war; he can only prolong it.</u> . . . A criminal regime cannot achieve a German victory. Separate yourselves in time from everything connected with National Socialism. In the aftermath a terrible but just judgment will be meted out to those who stayed in hiding, who were cowardly and hesitant.

By now, the fortunes of war had turned against Hitler and his once-invincible armies.

British and American warplanes were dropping bombs called "blockbusters" on German cities almost nightly, shaking the earth and smashing buildings as men, women, and children huddled in air-raid shelters and cellars. On the eastern front, stiffening resistance and the ferocious cold of the Russian winter had halted the German advance into the Soviet Union. Hitler's armies were sinking into mud and snow. On February 3, 1943, the Germans, encircled by the Russian army at the city of Stalingrad, surrendered after suffering enormous casualties. Out of 420,000 German troops, only 90,000 remained.

Enraged by the horrific loss of life at Stalingrad, Kurt Huber insisted on writing the sixth leaflet himself: "Shaken and broken, our people behold the loss of the men of Stalingrad. Three hundred and thirty thousand German men have been senselessly and irresponsibly driven to death and destruction by the inspired strategy of our World War I Private First Class. Führer, we thank you!"

The fifth and sixth leaflets were printed in much greater numbers than the first four. The group's new mimeograph machine still had to be cranked by hand, however, and leaflets folded

German troops fought a losing battle from trenches dug into the Russian snow, March 1942.

into stamped envelopes. Working in shifts night after night in Eickemeyer's cellar, the students produced several thousand leaflets.

Hans, Sophie, Alex, Traute, Willi, and others took turns as couriers, carrying backpacks and suitcases filled with leaflets to distant towns by train, then mailing the leaflets to still other cities, so that they would not be postmarked in the place where they appeared. Those mailed in Stuttgart were delivered in Frankfurt, while those sent from Vienna were received in Salzburg, creating the impression that the resistance movement was much bigger than it actually was. At the same time, hundreds of loose leaflets were left at night in telephone booths, on parked cars, in the lobbies of apartment buildings.

The couriers knew that the police could search the luggage on a train at any time. When they boarded the train in Munich, they would hoist the suitcase or backpack up into the luggage rack in one car, then move far down the train to sit out the journey in another car. If the police conducted a search and discovered the leaflets, they could not know to whom they belonged.

When the couriers reached their destination, they would retrieve the leaflets and set out

German prisoners of war following the Battle of Stalingrad,
Germany's first major defeat of World War II, February 1943.

into the night, walking down empty, blacked-out wartime streets, looking for out-of-the-way mailboxes. And when their suitcases were finally empty, they would board a train back to Munich.

They traveled alone, never in pairs, just in case they were caught. If questioned, they always had a well-rehearsed story to explain why they were traveling, as well as all the required identity papers in good order to hand over to a questioning police officer.

Even with these precautions, the sight of a uniformed policeman approaching down a crowded train aisle or on an unfamiliar street in a strange town was an encounter calling for steel nerves. The couriers had to submit to scrutiny

The Gestapo chief Meinrich Muller. He ordered an urgent manhunt to find the authors of the White Rose leaflets.

without trembling, to appear cool and distant, eyes blank, face expressionless, even though they might be terrified. They knew that each trip could be their last.

When Sophie stopped off at Ulm to visit her parents during one of these trips, she could not resist the urge to show a leaflet to her father. She told him she had "found" it in Munich. Robert Scholl read it with interest and remarked that it was an encouraging sign of resistance. Then he turned to his daughter with a troubled expression and said, "Sophie, I hope you and Hans haven't anything to do with this."

"How can you even think of such a thing?" Sophie replied. "Things are brewing all over Munich, but we don't get involved in them."

While Professor Huber was busy writing the sixth leaflet, Hans, Alex, and Willi were carrying out their riskiest action so far. Venturing into the blacked-out streets of Munich late at night, they took turns: one would stand guard with a loaded pistol while the other two painted anti-Nazi slogans on the walls of the university and other public buildings. Using black tar-based paint that was hard to remove, they painted "FREEDOM!," "DOWN WITH HITLER!," and "HITLER THE MASS MURDERER!" They added swastikas — the Nazi symbol — crossed out with smears of paint.

Sophie discovered the graffiti on her way to class one morning. A crowd gathered at the main entrance to the university was watching two Russian women laborers trying to scrub the three-foot-high black letters of "FREEDOM!" off a wall as a guard stood by. Sophie suspected that Hans was involved, and when she asked, "You did that, didn't you?" he nodded. She wanted to take part in the graffiti operation, but Hans was absolutely opposed. It was too dangerous, he argued.

The leaflets circulating in German cities and the slogans painted on Munich walls were now the target of an urgent Gestapo investigation. A special task force had been established to hunt down the authors of the leaflets and bring about their "speedy arrest." A reward was offered to anyone who could identify those responsible.

"I always understood," Alex would explain, "that I could lose my life in the event of an investigation. I ignored this all because my deep urge to combat National Socialism was stronger."

The university's light-filled *Lichthof,* or atrium, with its glass-domed ceiling.

SEVEN

ARRESTED

ON the morning of Thursday, February 18, 1943, Hans and Sophie left their student rooms at Number 13 Franz-Joseph-Strasse and set out for the university a few blocks away. Hans was carrying a large suitcase packed with about fifteen hundred leaflets. Sophie carried a briefcase holding a few hundred more.

Following their familiar path to the campus, they turned south on Leopoldstrasse, a wide boulevard lined on both sides by tall poplar trees. They walked by the Academy of Fine Arts on their right and passed the monumental Victory Arch on their left, straddling the boulevard, crowned by a statue of a female Bavaria driving a chariot drawn by four lions.

They crossed University Square, entered the main building, and

Carrying a suitcase packed with leaflets, Hans and Sophie walked past this fountain in University Square, went through one of the arches at the university entrance, and climbed a short flight of stairs to the skylighted atrium, or entry hall.

Number 13 Franz Joseph Strasse in Munich, where Hans and Sophie Scholl lived as students.

climbed a short flight of stairs to the vast marble entry hall. It was flooded with sunlight pouring from the great glass-domed ceiling three stories above. A giant stone staircase led to the upper floors and a circular gallery just below the glass dome.

The entrance hall was empty and quiet. Hans and Sophie had planned to reach the campus while students were still in class, behind the closed doors of their lecture halls. They would distribute the leaflets throughout the building while classes were in session, then slip away without being detected.

They were convinced that the time had come when students would be receptive to their call for resistance. Rumbles of discontent were surfacing more and more often across German society. After the military disaster at Stalingrad, it was rumored that even the army was turning against Hitler. And in Munich just a month earlier, students had staged an angry demonstration to protest offensive remarks by Paul Giesler, governor of Bavaria and a high-ranking Nazi official.

Speaking at a mass assembly marking the 470th anniversary of the university's founding, Giesler had launched a tirade against students who kept their noses in books while a war was going on. "Falsely clever minds," he said, were not an expression of "real life." Then he added: "Real life is transmitted to us only by Adolf Hitler, with his light, joyful, life-affirming teachings!"

Many of the male students, Giesler charged, were shirkers using their studies as an excuse for draft dodging. And he singled out female students for his most biting criticism. "As for the girls," he suggested, "the natural place for a woman is not at the university, but with her family, at the side of her husband." Instead of studying, women should be using their "healthy bodies" to produce babies for the Fatherland. "And for those women students not pretty enough to catch a man," he said with a leer, "I'd be happy to lend them one of my assistants."

Giesler's remarks were met with a rising chorus of hisses, boos, whistles, and shouts. As outraged members of the audience got up to leave, scuffles and fistfights broke out with the storm troopers who tried to hold them back. Dozens of students were arrested on the spot. Hundreds more poured into the streets. Linking arms, men and women students together marched down the boulevard singing and shouting in an open

Paul Giesler. His insulting remarks about women students incited a riot at Munich University.

display of political protest that had never been seen before in Nazi Germany. A state of emergency was declared in Munich. Telephone service was suspended. Radio broadcasts were silenced.

The sixth White Rose leaflet, written by Kurt Huber, was addressed to "Fellow Students!" It blamed Hitler, "the most abominable tyrant our people have ever been forced to endure," for the bloodbath at Stalingrad. It condemned the Nazis for trying "to drug us, to revolutionize us, to regiment us in the most promising young years of our lives. 'Philosophical training' is the name given to the despicable method by which our budding intellectual development is muffled in a fog of empty phrases." And the leaflet denounced Paul Giesler for his "lewd jokes," which "insult the honor of the women students." Declaring, "The day of reckoning has come," the leaflet called on German youth to "finally rise, take revenge, and atone, smash its tormentors, and set up a new Europe of the spirit."

Hans and Sophie began to distribute copies of this leaflet. Working separately and systematically, they moved up and down the empty hallways, depositing batches of leaflets by the closed doors of lecture halls. They left more leaflets all around the entrance hall, on the landings of the great staircase, on marble shelves and windowsills, rushing to finish before classes ended. Finally, Sophie scooped up the remaining leaflets from their suitcase and, on an impulse, flung them into the air and watched as they fluttered down to the empty hall below.

As the leaflets were falling, a janitor named Jakob Schmid came into the building. He picked up a leaflet, took one look, then spotted Hans and Sophie three stories above. "Stop!" he yelled. "Stop! You're under arrest!" Just then, the doors to the lecture halls opened and students poured out into the corridors. Still shouting, Schmid dashed up the stairs, elbowing students aside, as Hans and Sophie, who was now holding the empty suitcase, tried to lose themselves in the surging crowd. But Schmid managed to grab Hans's arm. Sophie stayed by her brother's side, seemingly calm. With so many eyewitnesses swarming around them, it made no sense to try to escape. They would have to talk their way out of trouble.

Schmid led Hans and Sophie to the office of the university rector (president). Students in the corridors milled around nervously, some picking up leaflets and reading them, others dropping

The balcony from which Sophie tossed a handful of White Rose leaflets down into the entry hall.

them hurriedly after one look. By now, an alarm had been sounded. All exits from the building had been locked.

In less than thirty minutes, a team of Gestapo agents arrived, headed by Robert Mohr, the agent in charge of the White Rose investigation. At first, Mohr felt that Schmid, the janitor, must have made a mistake. It did not seem possible

Soviet troops examine a collection of handcuffs and leg shackles at the former Gestapo headquarters in Berlin, 1945.

that the well-mannered, clean-cut brother and sister sitting so calmly in the rector's office could be part of a movement to overthrow the government. Mohr examined their identification papers. Everything was in order — they were enrolled as legitimate students at the university. Why were they carrying an empty suitcase? They were about to go home to Ulm, Sophie explained matter-of-factly, and they intended to bring clean laundry and fresh clothing back to Munich.

As the questioning continued, Hans realized that he was carrying Christoph Probst's handwritten draft of a new leaflet in his coat pocket. When the Gestapo agents had their backs turned, he quietly removed the paper and, holding it under his chair, began to rip it into pieces. But he was spotted doing this, and the scraps of paper were retrieved. Hans explained that the paper had been handed to him by a student he didn't know. He had no idea what was written on it, he said, and he feared it might incriminate him if he was arrested.

Gestapo agents were scouring the building, gathering leaflets scattered throughout the corridors, on the staircase, and in the entrance hall. When every last leaflet had been collected, they were brought to the rector's office, stacked in neat piles, and placed in the suitcase and Sophie's briefcase. They fit perfectly.

Mohr ordered that Hans and Sophie be handcuffed and taken to Gestapo headquarters for further questioning. A fellow student, Christa Meyer-Heidkamp, recalled their departure:

All university exits were blocked. The students were instructed to assemble in the atrium [entry hall]. Each of us who had taken a leaflet had to turn it over to a specifically designated collector. We stood there waiting for two hours. Finally Hans Scholl and his sister were led past us in handcuffs. He looked at us for the last time, but no muscle in his face revealed any recognition. He was aware that this would betray any fellow student familiar to him to the Gestapo.

Hans and Sophie were bundled into a waiting Gestapo van and driven away.

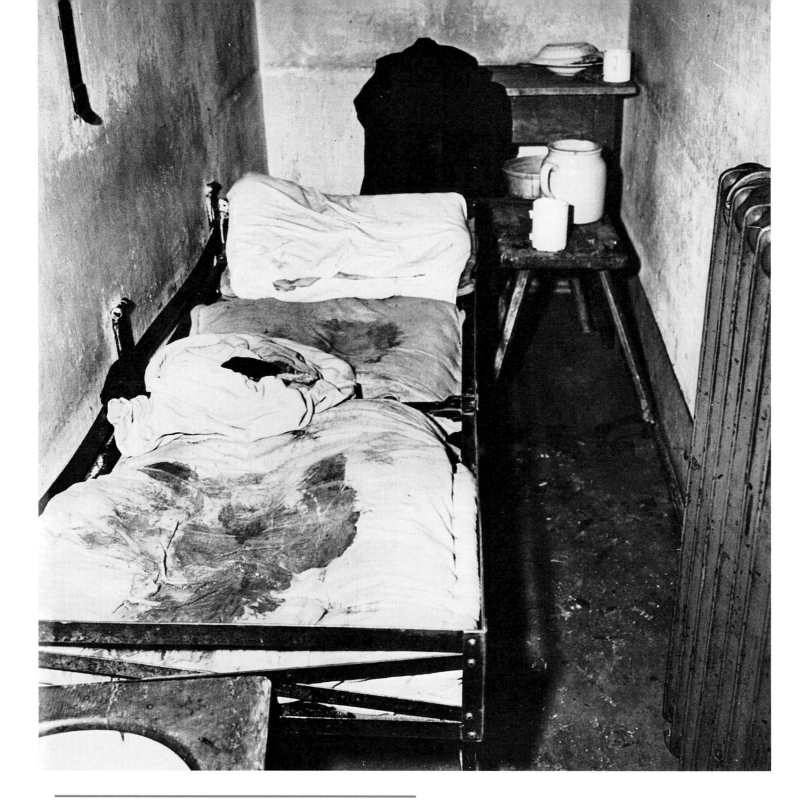

A cell in a Gestapo prison where a female prisoner died after a beating.
Her clothing lies in the center of the bloodstained bed.

* * * * EIGHT * * * *

"LONG LIVE FREEDOM!"

HANS and Sophie were held at Gestapo headquarters for four days. They were interrogated separately day and night, for hours at a time, and were not allowed to see visitors or have contact with each other.

They insisted at first that they knew nothing about the White Rose leaflets. The janitor, they said, had been mistaken. Standing in the entrance hall, looking up into the sun streaming through the glass dome of the ceiling three stories above, he could not have been sure who had thrown the leaflets. With so many students pouring out of lecture halls and milling about the corridors and staircase, he was confused and went after the wrong suspects. Hans and Sophie told their version of the story with such cool conviction that Robert Mohr, the chief interrogator, was inclined to believe them.

Gestapo agents, meanwhile, were searching their rooms on Franz-Josef-Strasse. They found hundreds of unused postage stamps and envelopes, personal letters, and Sophie's handwritten account book, containing many names and listing expenditures for supplies and equipment. Inquiries in the neighborhood led the Gestapo to Eickemeyer's studio, where the leaflets had been produced. There they found the students' typewriter and mimeograph machine, and the paint and brushes used to smear anti-Hitler slogans on university walls.

Gestapo agents also managed to piece together the shredded leaflet Hans had tried to destroy. The handwriting matched that on a letter from Christoph Probst found in Hans's room. By Friday, February 19, Christoph had been arrested. Hans and Sophie did not know that he was being held and interrogated in the same building.

Confronted with so much evidence, Hans and Sophie each realized that their situation was hopeless. They knew now that they were not going to talk their way out of trouble. In an effort to protect Christoph and divert suspicion from their other comrades, they changed their stories, admitting everything. They each took full responsibility for the writing and distribution of

the leaflets. The White Rose campaign, they now insisted, had been conceived and carried out by just the two of them.

Robert Mohr tried to persuade Sophie to say that she did not agree with Hans, that she had gone along with him without understanding the consequences of their actions. Sophie refused to make any such statement. She told Mohr that she had not been misled by her brother. She understood exactly what she doing. "I would do it all over again — because I'm not wrong," she said. "*You* have the wrong worldview."

Mohr could not help being impressed by the conduct of his two prisoners: "Until the bitter end," he reported, "Sophie and Hans Scholl managed a bearing that must be called unique. Both [said] . . . that their activities had only one purpose, preventing an even greater calamity from overtaking Germany and, if possible, helping to save the lives of hundreds of thousands of German soldiers and people. . . . [They] were convinced that their sacrifice was not in vain."

High-ranking Nazi officials were demanding an immediate trial and conviction. They were determined to make an example of Hans, Sophie, Christoph, and all those who had conspired with them.

Nazi judge Roland Freisler, seated under the swastika, questions a standing defendant during a session of the People's Court.

On Monday, February 22, 1943, at 10:00 a.m. — four days after the initial arrests — Sophie, Hans, and Christoph were brought before a session of the so-called People's Court at the Palace of Justice in Munich. These special courts had been established not to administer justice, but to eradicate enemies of the Nazi regime. The courtroom was packed that morning with an invited audience of Nazi Party officials, storm troopers, and members of the armed forces. No family members or friends of the accused were allowed to attend the trial.

Roland Freisler, president of the People's Court. Known as the "hanging judge," he preferred to sentence convicted defendants to death at the guillotine.

The indictment charged the defendants with "treasonable aid to the enemy, preparations for high treason, and demoralization of the troops." There would be no witnesses for the defense. The trial would be based solely on the evidence collected by the Gestapo during the previous four days. Throughout the three-and-a-half-hour trial, the court-appointed defense attorneys sat silently in their chairs. They did not make a single effort on behalf of the defendants they were assigned to represent.

The presiding judge, Roland Freisler, was notorious for his courtroom theatrics and his merciless bullying of those unfortunate enough to appear before him. When Freisler pronounced a death sentence, which was often, he would pause for dramatic effect, make a slicing motion with his arm, then shout, "Off with his head!" The guillotine was Hitler's favored method of executing political prisoners.

Freisler swept into the courtroom draped in crimson robes trimmed in gold, with a red cap atop his bald head. Three assistant judges trailed behind him. As they entered, the spectators leaped to their feet, extended their right arms, and shouted, *"Heil Hitler!"*

The defendants were told to stand while the

charges against them were read aloud to the court. Later they were allowed to offer their brief version of events. Freisler listened impatiently, constantly interrupting, "ranting and raging, screaming with his voice cracking, and jumping to his feet time and again," a spectator reported. "Throughout the trial he conducted himself like a prosecutor rather than a judge."

Sophie defended her actions. She expressed no regrets. "What we have said and what we have written is what so many people believe, only they don't dare speak up," she told the judge, refusing to bow to his bullying remarks.

When it was Hans's turn to speak, he asked Freisler for a lenient sentence for Christoph, who, he said, had virtually nothing to do with the leaflet campaign. "If you have nothing to say for yourself," the judge told him, "then kindly keep your mouth shut!"

Christoph himself asked for clemency because his wife was ill and his three children would be left fatherless if he were executed.

The verdict was never in doubt. At 1:30 p.m., after a brief recess, Judge Freisler announced that the defendants had been found guilty. All three had been sentenced to death by the guillotine. For opposing Hitler, they would lose their lives. Any lesser penalty, Freisler told the court, would weaken public support for the war.

As the verdict was being read, the proceedings were interrupted by a commotion at the courtroom door. Robert and Magdalene Scholl and their younger son, Werner, on army leave from the Russian front, were demanding to be admitted. Robert Scholl was struggling with the guards, who were trying to hold him back. Judge Freisler ordered the guards to evict the family. As they were being shoved out the door, Robert shouted, "There is a higher law before which we all must stand!"

Werner, who was wearing his army uniform, managed to slip back in after the verdict was read and the spectators were leaving. Tearfully, he embraced his brother and sister. "Stay strong," Hans told him, "no compromises."

Immediately after the trial, the three defendants were transported to Munich's Stadelheim prison. In a desperate last attempt to see their children, Robert and Magdalene rushed to the prison, where sympathetic guards broke the rules and allowed the family a brief final visit. Hans was brought into the dimly lit reception room first. He thanked his parents for giving him life, and for their love and support. "I have no hatred

Stadelheim prison in Munich, where Sophie Scholl, Christoph Probst, and Hans Scholl were beheaded.

for anyone anymore," he told them. "I have put all that behind me."

"You will go down in history," his father replied. "There is such a thing as justice despite this. I am proud of both of you."

Hans asked his parents to remember him to his friends. As he mentioned one last name, he bowed his head and wept. Quickly, he composed himself, embraced his parents, and was led out of the room.

Sophie was brought in next. As she entered the room, she smiled at her parents. "Do you want some candy?" her mother asked, as though this were an ordinary meeting on a day like any other.

"Oh, yes, of course," Sophie replied. "I didn't have any lunch."

Magdalene took her daughter's hands and said, "Sophie, Sophie — so now you will never again set foot in our house."

"Oh, what do those few short years matter, Mother?" Sophie replied. She paused, then added, "We took the blame, for everything. That is bound to have its effect in time to come."

Robert Mohr found Sophie sobbing when he went to her cell after the family visit. "I've just said goodbye to my parents," she said. "I'm sure you understand." Mohr was shaken. He tried to offer a few comforting words. He wrote later that he had been deeply affected by Sophie's courage, and by her faith in God.

Christoph had no chance to see his family at the end. His wife was not yet out of the hospital after giving birth to their third child.

At 4:00 p.m. that afternoon, Hans, Sophie, and Christoph were taken one after another to the prison office. They stood before the chief prosecutor, seated at a large table, as he read aloud the official declaration sentencing them to death. There would be no act of clemency. The executions would begin at exactly 5:00 p.m.

"They bore themselves with marvelous bravery," a prison guard told Inge Scholl. "The whole prison was impressed by them. That is why we risked bringing the three of them together once more — at the last moment before execution. If our act had become known, the consequences for us would have been severe. . . . It was just a few minutes that they had together, but I believe that it meant a great deal for them."

The prison chaplain went to their cells to administer the last rites and read passages from the Bible. From the Gospel of Saint John, he read: "Greater love hath no man than this, that a man lay down his life for his friends."

At 5:00 p.m., Sophie was led to the execution chamber. The executioner, a man named Johann Reichart, was waiting for her. He wore a long black coat, a white shirt, a black bow tie, a tall black top hat, and spotless white gloves. He stood beside the guillotine, a tall wooden frame from which a razor-sharp blade was suspended. Two guards on either side of Sophie held her in place. Five seconds after she entered the chamber, the blade was released. It dropped with a dull thud. Sophie Scholl was dead at the age of twenty-one.

Hans followed her into the chamber. He was twenty-four.

Finally, Christoph, twenty-three and the father of three, was beheaded.

Sophie and Christoph went silently to their deaths. But Hans could not resist a final act of defiance. Just before they positioned his head on the block, he called out, "Long live freedom!"

The interior of a Gestapo prison. More than a hundred people were arrested and imprisoned during the Gestapo investigation of the White Rose leaflet campaign.

★ ★ ★ ★ NINE ★ ★ ★ ★

A VOICE FROM WITHIN

HANS, Sophie, and Christoph were dead, but their voices could not be silenced. Within days of their execution, a new slogan appeared on the walls of Munich University: "SCHOLL LIVES! YOU CAN BREAK THE BODY BUT NEVER THE SPIRIT!"

The arrests continued. Alexander Schmorell, Willi Graf, and Professor Kurt Huber were taken into custody shortly after Hans and Sophie were arrested. One by one, more than one hundred other suspects were swept up by the Gestapo dragnet, some simply because they were friends or family members of the accused. Under the Nazi policy of *Sippenhaft,* or clan arrest, the parents, spouses, siblings, and children of "political criminals" were held jointly responsible for acts of resistance.

The surviving members of the Scholl family were arrested — all except

Werner, who had been sent back to active duty on the Russian front (where he was killed in action). Elisabeth was soon released due to poor health, but Mrs. Scholl and Inge were held in solitary confinement and interrogated for four months before they were let go. The women were acquitted at the Scholl family trial in August 1943, while Robert Scholl was sentenced to two years of hard labor.

Professor Huber's wife and sister, who knew practically nothing about the White Rose, were jailed. His twelve-year-old daughter was placed under Gestapo supervision and instructed to tell anyone who asked that her parents were away on a trip.

On April 19, 1943, the People's Court reconvened in Munich for the second trial of White Rose dissidents. Kurt Huber, Alexander Schmorell, and Willi Graf had been indicted as active participants in the leaflet campaign. Eleven other defendants were charged with helping distribute leaflets or "having been aware of this act of high treason but having failed to report it." Most of the accused were students in their early twenties; four were teenagers. Nazi dignitaries again packed the courtroom and again Judge Roland Freisler presided. "Anyone who endangers the National Socialism way of life is guilty of high treason and deserves to die," he announced.

After a fourteen-hour trial, Alex Schmorell, Willi Graf, and Professor Huber were sentenced to death by the guillotine. Ten defendants received prison terms, and one was acquitted. Nazi propaganda minister Joseph Goebbels had instructed Judge Freisler to go easy on the death sentences, because, as Goebbels said, the earlier "Munich sentences had not been accepted with much understanding by the public."

Alex Schmorell and Kurt Huber were beheaded on July 13, 1943. Their appeals for clemency had been rejected by personal order of Adolf Hitler. "I'm going with the awareness that I followed my deepest convictions and the truth," Alex wrote to his parents. "This allows me to meet my hour of death with a conscience at peace."

Willi Graf was held in solitary confinement for seven months and interrogated daily in a futile attempt to pry from him the names of other White Rose members. Willi gave up no names. On October 12, 1943, he followed his friends into the execution chamber.

More arrests, more trials, and more executions took place in the months that followed. "The [Nazi] party has to break terror with tenfold

A session of the People's Court. The defendant, standing before the judges, was accused of being involved in a failed attempt on Hitler's life. She was executed.

terror," Hitler declared. "It has to extinguish the traitors — whoever they are, whatever their disguise." But even as the Gestapo tried to crush every sign of dissent, a new version of the White Rose leaflets was circulating in Germany and beyond. It proclaimed in bold type: "DESPITE EVERYTHING, THEIR SPIRIT LIVES ON!"

"I will never forget the excitement when a leaflet was pressed into my hand in the editorial room of the [newspaper] *Allgemeine Zeitung*," a

German journalist recalled. "The leaflets were being circulated by White Rose followers in Hamburg. Something inflammatory, heartening — yes, magical! — emanating from these typewritten and [duplicated] lines. We copied them and passed them on. A wave of enthusiasm swept over us — we who risked so damned little in comparison."

Word of the leaflets filtered into the concentration camps, bringing a glimmer of hope. Copies were smuggled into Sweden and Switzerland, neutral nations not under the Nazi yoke, and from there found their way to London. By the end of 1943, British warplanes were dropping White Rose leaflets by the tens of thousands over Germany's cities and towns. They were headed in bold type A GERMAN LEAFLET: MANIFESTO OF THE MUNICH STUDENTS. In this way, the voices of the White Rose student resisters were now reaching millions of people in both Nazi-occupied territory and the free world.

From the United States, in a wartime broadcast of the federal government's Voice of America, the exiled German novelist and Nobel Prize laureate Thomas Mann hailed the White Rose students: "Gallant, glorious young people! You have not died in vain. You will not be forgotten."

By the summer of 1944, German forces were on the defensive across Europe. Russian armies on the eastern front and an allied British-French-American force in the west were closing in on Hitler's Third Reich (third empire), as the Nazis called it.

In August, the Allies liberated Paris. In March 1945, Russian troops linked up with American forces on the Elbe River. Hitler retreated to his bunker in the ruins of bombed-out Berlin. On April 30, he committed suicide, and on May 7, Germany surrendered.

During the final days of the war, the remaining White Rose prisoners, many awaiting execution, were freed by advancing Allied troops. One member of the Hamburg group, Heinz Kucharski, sentenced to death on April 20, 1945, when the Allies were deep inside Germany, managed to escape from his captors during an air raid while he was being transported to the execution site.

✳ ✳ ✳

"What we did will make waves," Sophie had told her parents at their farewell meeting. Today, the members of the White Rose are counted among the legendary heroes of World War II. Books have been written and movies made about them. An opera titled *The White Rose* has been performed to

After more than four years of Nazi occupation, a jubilant crowd celebrates the liberation of Paris by Allied troops led by Free French General Charles de Gaulle and his forces, August 26, 1944. The commander of the German garrison defied an order by Hitler to blow up Paris landmarks and burn the city to the ground.

After laying down his sword, Field Marshal Wilhelm Keitel signs the ratified German surrender terms in Berlin, May 8, 1945. Although Germany had surrendered to the Allies a day earlier, Stalin had insisted on a second surrender ceremony in Berlin.

standing ovations at many of the world's leading opera houses. In Germany, hundreds of schools, squares, and streets are named in honor of the White Rose and its members.

At Munich University, the square outside the main entrance is now Geschwister-Scholl-Platz — Scholl Siblings Square. A unique memorial in front of the entrance is made of ceramic tiles depicting White Rose leaflets that appear to have been dropped onto the cobblestone pavement. The square across the street is named Professor-Huber-Platz.

Inside the sunlit entrance hall, where the janitor Jacob Schmid saw leaflets falling from a third-floor balcony, a bronze bust of Sophie Scholl is usually festooned with fresh flowers. The White Rose Museum, just off the entrance hall, was founded in 1987 by surviving members and relatives pledged to keep the spirit of the White Rose alive. The museum is staffed by volunteers of the White Rose Foundation. The exhibit tells the story of the student resistance movement through photographs and displays — diaries, letters, and personal belongings of White Rose members, including Hans's typewriter.

Here, visitors from all over the world come to pay their respects to the brave idealists who felt compelled to resist when so many others chose to conform or simply look away. "It makes me wonder," said a sixteen-year-old visitor from York, Pennsylvania, "whether people would stand up for something they feel is right in our generation."

For members of the White Rose, resistance was a matter of conscience.

"I acted as I had to act," Kurt Huber said at his trial, "prompted by a voice that came from within."

"I'm searching for myself, just myself," Hans had written years earlier, "because this much I do know: I'll only find the truth inside me."

And Sophie wrote: "We carry all our standards

Munich's University Square is today named Geschwister-Scholl-Platz (Scholl Siblings Square).

The White Rose memorial at the entrance to Munich University. Ceramic tiles on the cobblestone pavement depict scattered White Rose leaflets.

within ourselves, only we don't look for them closely enough. Perhaps because they are the severest standards."

* * *

We are told that the Christian martyr Saint Denis, after being beheaded around A.D. 250, picked up his head and walked several miles while preaching a sermon the entire way, a feat that has always been regarded as a miracle.

The story of the White Rose movement and its decapitated martyrs tells us that miracles still occur. We hear their voices even today, speaking truth to power. They will not be silent.

Sophie Scholl at seventeen, summer 1938: "I can never look at
a limpid stream without at least dangling my feet in it."

✶✶✶✶✶ SOURCE NOTES ✶✶✶✶✶

1. Embraced by the Hitler Youth

1   "Don't believe them . . . shamefully."
Scholl, 6

2   "We entered . . . approve." Scholl, 6

"We heard . . . enthusiasm." Scholl, 5–7

3   "inferior." Bartoletti, 25 and 42

5   "Ulm . . . cathedral." Scholl, 5

6–7   "For we loved . . . couldn't say why." Scholl, 5–6

7   "I can never . . . grateful." Vinke, 28

7–9   "Hans was . . . dangerous." Axelrod, 33–34

9   "Your Hans . . . *Stamm*." Axelrod, 45

We'll go . . . whole world. Dumbach, 29

"It seems . . . Führer speaks." Dumbach, 32

2. Rumblings of Doubt

11   "When [Hans] returned . . . disappointment."
Scholl, 8

"sensible conversation." Dumbach, 33

12   "Jewish filth." McDonough, 36

"You don't need . . . the manuals." Scholl, 10;
also in McDonough, 36; Hanser, 50

"We hardly had . . . barking out orders."
McDonough, 41

14   "Our communal . . . the name!" Jens, 3

"What is . . . Göring!" Hanser, 63

15   "the wisest of my women." Dumbach, 38

17   "very serious . . . fun-loving." Axelrod, 33

"She danced . . . her partner." Vinke, 56

17   "degenerate." Dumbach, 38

"He who doesn't . . . literature." Vinke, 54

"Where one . . . people." Berenbaum, xxxiii

"Why can't . . . member?" Vinke, 42

"She just . . . racism." Vinke, 42

"Father . . . went through?" Scholl, 11

18 "What did . . . crime." Scholl, 11

"There awoke . . . hold of us." Scholl, 11

"We have a large . . . collectively." Dumbach, 43

19 "In the home . . . or not." McDonough, 34

"This place . . . expression." Jens, 2

3. Half Soldier, Half Student

21 "My parents . . . happen." Vinke, 50–51

22 "Thank you . . . pride again." Jens, 5

"Hans Scholl . . . care of it." Vinke, 53

"subversive activities." Jens, 7 & 10

"a close relationship." McDonough, 45.
This is apparently the only documented
instance of homosexual activity by Hans. At
Munich University, he engaged in romantic
relationships with a succession of women,
most significantly Traute Lafrenz. His
sexuality remains a matter of conjecture.
See McDonough, 41–50 and 107

"I'm not afraid . . . myself." Jens, 10

"youthful exuberance . . . failing."
McDonough, 49

"I often . . . university." Jens, 7

23 "totally unjustified." McDonough, 46

"If those bastards . . . shoot him." Vinke, 54

"had deliberately . . . no return." Shirer, 434, as
quoted by Hanser, 78

24 "softhearted squeamishness." Shirer, 434, as
quoted by Hanser, 78

"The cowed . . . snake." Shirer, 434, as
quoted by Hanser, 78

25 "It was . . . hospital." Scholl, 17

26 "No one . . . everywhere." Scholl, 17

"You and your men . . . sake." Jens, 36

"Close your . . . compassion!" Hanser, 84

26–27 "We've commandeered . . . goes on." Jens,
51

28 "The children . . . self-centered." Jens,
72–73

29 "I doubt . . . poison." Jens, 146

4. Leaflets of the White Rose

31 "It seems . . . tomorrow." Scholl, 22

"I can still . . . expectation." Scholl, 26

"crisp . . . cake." Scholl, 22

32 "Tonight . . . friends," Scholl, 26

"degenerate art." Hanser, 52

"When he . . . whole being." Scholl, 21–22

33 "He was . . . concentration camps." Müller,
29

"All at once . . . under a spell." Scholl, 28

33–34 "They would . . . time to time." Scholl, 22

34 "You had . . . talk to them." Axelrod, 50

34–36 "permissible . . . incurable disease." Scholl,
19–20

36 "Finally a man . . . machine." Scholl, 20

"What I seek . . . inside me." Jens, 42

"There's something . . . to be right." Jens, 202

37   "There's nothing more . . . resisting?" Scholl, 30

38–39   "Is it not . . . subhuman." Excerpt from the translated transcript of Leaflet #1, issued by the White Rose Museum.

39   "The name . . . political program." McDonough, 97

     "I could tell . . . done it." Vinke, 119

     "It's not a good . . . endangered." McDonough, 98

41   "She knew . . . way back." Scholl, 34

41   "They could . . . throw bombs." Vinke, 108

5. "We Are Your Bad Conscience"

45   "Since the conquest . . . guilty!" Leaflet #2, Müller, 45

45–46   "dictatorship of evil . . . ideology." Leaflet #3, Müller, 50

46   "Every word . . . leave you in peace!" Leaflet #4, Müller, 51–52

47–48   "Hans went off . . . them all." Jens, 209

49   "The misery . . . again." Dumbach, 98

     "The city . . . all of us." Jens, 216

     "Russia is so vast . . . boundless too." Jens, 216

     "Asiatic inferiors . . . harshness." Hanser, 177

     "We have . . . around us." Hanser, 178

"ripped apart . . . we love it." Dumbach, 101

50   "We went . . . peacetime." Jens, 214

     "God's scourge . . . two years." McDonough, 85

     "malicious slander of the Führer." Vinke, 122

     "politically unreliable." Jens, 257

     "Even though . . . gray cell." Jens, 217

51   "I marvel . . . in Germany." Jens, 239

6. "Down with Hitler!"

53   "standing over . . . depressing." Jens, 211

53–54   "delightful . . . human beings." Jens, 244

54   "Thoughts . . . are free!" en.wikipedia.org/wiki/Die_Gedanken_sind_frei

55   "No family . . . our families." Axelrod, 75

     "I'm never . . . uttered." Jens, 255

     "Life . . . danger." Bartoletti, 124

57   "The war is . . . cowardly and hesitant." Leaflet #5, Müller, 53

     "Shaken and broken . . . thank you!" Excerpt from Leaflet #6, Müller, 54

60   "Sophie, I hope . . . in them." Dumbach, 128; also in Vinke, 139

61   "You did that didn't you?" McDonough, 114

     "speedy arrest." McDonough, 113

     "I always . . . stronger." McDonough, 97

7. Arrested

65   "Falsely clever minds . . . my assistants."
McDonough, 111; Dumbach, 131–32;
Hanser, 202

66   "Fellow Students! . . . Europe of the spirit."
Leaflet #6, Müller, 54

"Stop! . . . arrest!" McDonough, 122

69   "All university exits . . . Gestapo." Müller, 42

8. "Long Live Freedom!"

72   "I would . . . worldview." Dumbach, 151

"Until the bitter end . . . not in vain." Vinke,
166

74   "treasonable aid . . . troops." Müller, 58

"Off with his head!" McDonough, 141

75   "ranting and raging . . . judge." Müller, 58

"What we . . . speak up." Scholl, 59, and
Müller, 58

"If you have . . . mouth shut!" McDonough,
143; also in Dumbach, 158

"There is . . . must stand!" Scholl, 59

"Stay strong . . . compromises." Dumbach,
159; also in Scholl, 60

75–76   "I have . . . both of you." McDonough, 148;
also in Scholl, 61

76–77   "Do you want . . . time to come." Dumbach,
160; also in Scholl, 61–62

77   "I've just . . . understand." McDonough, 149

"They bore themselves . . . deal for them."
Scholl, 62

"Greater love . . . friends." John 15:13, King
James Version

"Long live freedom!" Scholl, 62

9. A Voice from Within

79   "SCHOLL LIVES! . . . THE SPIRIT."
Dumbach, 153; *New York Times,* "Nazi Slur
Stirred Students' Revolt," April 18, 1943

80   "having been aware . . . report it." Müller, 58

"Anyone . . . deserves to die." Hanser, 265

"Munich . . . the public": Muller, 58.

"I'm going . . . at peace." Dumbach, 177–78

80–81   "The [Nazi] party . . . disguise." Dumbach,
163

81   "DESPITE EVERYTHING . . . LIVES ON!"
Hanser, 281

81–82   "I will never . . . comparison." Hanser, 282

82   "A GERMAN . . . STUDENTS." Hanser, 281

"Gallant, glorious . . . forgotten." Hanser,
282

"What we did will make waves." Hanser, 281

85   "It makes me . . . our generation." White
Rose Foundation leaflet, "Bring the White
Rose Exhibition to Your Community."

"I acted . . . within." Hanser, 270

"I'm searching . . . inside me." Jens, 42

85–87   "We carry . . . standards." Vinke, 211

✳✳✳✳✳✳ SELECTED BIBLIOGRAPHY ✳✳✳✳✳✳

Books

Axelrod, Toby. *Hans and Sophie Scholl: German Resisters of the White Rose.* Irvine, Calif.: Saddleback Publishing, 2000.

Bartoletti, Susan Campbell. *Hitler Youth: Growing Up in Hitler's Shadow.* New York: Scholastic, 2005.

Berenbaum, Michael. *Witness to the Holocaust: An Illustrated Documentary History of the Holocaust in the Words of Its Victims, Perpetrators and Bystanders.* New York: HarperCollins, 1997.

Dawidowicz, Lucy S. *The War Against the Jews, 1933–1945.* New York: Holt, Rinehart and Winston, 1975.

Dumbach, Annette, and Jud Newborn. *Sophie Scholl and the White Rose.* Oxford, England: Oneworld Publications, 2007. First published in the United States as *Shattering the German Night.* Boston: Little Brown, 1986.

Giblin, James Cross. *The Life and Death of Adolf Hitler.* New York: Clarion Books, 2002.

Goldhagen, Daniel Jonah. *Hitler's Willing Executioners: Ordinary Germans and the Holocaust.* New York: Alfred A. Knopf, 1996.

Hanser, Richard. *A Noble Treason: The Story of Sophie Scholl and the White Rose Revolt Against Hitler.* San Francisco: Ignatius Press, 2012. First edition published by G. P. Putnam's Sons, New York, 1979.

Jens, Inge, ed. *At the Heart of the White Rose: Letters and Diaries of Hans and Sophie Scholl.* Translated from the German by J. Maxwell Brownjohn. New York: Harper & Row, 1987.

McDonough, Frank. *Sophie Scholl: The Real Story of the Woman Who Defied Hitler.* Stroud, Gloucestershire, U.K.: History Press, 2009.

Müller, Franz Joseph, et al. *The White Rose Exhibition on the Resistance by Students Against Hitler, Munich 1942/43.* Munich: The White Rose Foundation, 1991. The White Rose Museum exhibition catalog.

Scholl, Inge. *The White Rose: Munich, 1942–43.* Translated from the German by Arthur R. Schultz. Middletown, Conn.: Wesleyan University Press, 1983.

Shirer, William I. *The Rise and Fall of the Third Reich: A History of Nazi Germany.* New York: Simon and Schuster, 1960.

Vinke, Hermann. *The Short Life of Sophie Scholl.* Translated from the German by Hedwig Pachter. New York: Harper & Row, 1984.

Films

Sophie Scholl: The Final Days. Directed by Marc Rothemund, 2005. DVD, German with English subtitles. Academy Award nominee for best foreign language film.

The White Rose. Directed by Michael Verhoeven, 1982. VHS or DVD, German with English subtitles.

White Rose Museum Exhibition

"The Student Resistance Against Hitler, 1942/43," picturing the individuals of the White Rose, their path to resistance, actions, and persecution by the Nazi regime, is available for display across the United States. Contact weisse_rose_stiftung@yahoo.com.

Hans's portable typewriter.

✳✳✳✳✳✳ PICTURE CREDITS ✳✳✳✳✳✳

akg-images: 10, 13, 32, 73

akg-images/Voller Ernst/Chalde: 68

akg-images/interfoto: 6, 41, 54, 67, 88

akg-images/ullstein bild: opposite p. 1, 15, 30, 32 (left), 36

Evans Chan: 45, 62, 64 (2), 67, 85, 86, 97, 98

Library of Congress: 2, 3, 7, 8, 14, 18, 33, 50, 58, 81, 83, 84

National Archives: 4, 24, 25, 27, 42, 52

United States Holocaust Memorial Museum/Courtesy of Nancy & Michael Krzyzanowski, Solomon Bogard: 78

U.S. Holocaust Memorial Museum/Courtesy of Solomon Bogard: 70

U.S. Holocaust Memorial Museum/Courtesy of Fred Einstein: 35

U.S. Holocaust Memorial Museum/Courtesy of National Archives: 16, 23

U.S. Holocaust Memorial Museum/Courtesy of Henry Schwarzman: 56

U.S. Holocaust Memorial Museum/Courtesy of Laura Gillian Wood: 20

White Rose Museum: 40

Wikipedia/Creative Commons: 37, 76

Wikipedia/German Federal Archives: 28, 74

Wikipedia/public domain: 30, 38, 60

George (Jurgen) Wittenstein/akg: frontispiece, 33, 46, 47, 48, 51, 65

The White Rose Museum, located just off the university entry hall where Hans and Sophie were arrested.

★★★★★★ INDEX ★★★★★★

Note: Page numbers in **bold** refer to illustrations or captions.